Brannon Patterson was born on December 29, 1976, in Knoxville, TN. He is a single father to an amazing 12-year-old daughter. He has worked in varying management roles, primarily in the retail world, and has observed human behaviour at its worst and also at its very best. He views the world as an empath and tries to convey that in his writing style while maintaining a strong will and voice.

To my family, who have given me the kind of upbringing and perspective to think outside a structured box, and to my amazing daughter, Olivia, who even through the most basic decisions of my life is always my biggest factor and fan.

Brannon Patterson

Tales For The Trivial

AUSTIN MACAULEY PUBLISHERS™

LONDON • CAMBRIDGE • NEW YORK • SHARJAH

Ordering Information
Quantity sales: Special discounts are available on quantity purchases by corporations, associations, and others. For details, contact the publisher at the address below.

Publisher's Cataloging-in-Publication data
Patterson, Brannon
Tales For The Trivial

ISBN 9798889101543 (Paperback)
ISBN 9798889101550 (ePub e-book)

Library of Congress Control Number: 2023915692

www.austinmacauley.com/us

First Published 2024
Austin Macauley Publishers LLC
40 Wall Street, 33rd Floor, Suite 3302
New York, NY 10005
USA

mail-usa@austinmacauley.com
+1 (646) 5125767

I would like to extend a heartfelt thank you to Austin Macauley Publishers for taking this short story to publication.

What's the point, really? We are born; we learn the basics. We learn how to masterfully get some large version of ourselves to react to our every waking and resting need merely by being us. Sure, we cry, coo, and mess in our diapers to gain control over these people, but with each passing hour and every day, the caregivers in our lives seem like they will do anything to make us if not happy, then at least content. The kind of power a baby wields would be dangerous and corrupting in the hands of some of the most maniacal leaders throughout history. This power then shifts to the need to reach and pick ourselves up to move to obtain an object like a blanky, or to pull the ears of our favourite pet, or hey, how about that delicious-looking Gain pod? Still, for our continuously amazed and apparently easy to please parents, we are the absolute pinnacle of their universe. The undisputed champions of their worlds. As we obtain the autonomy of movement and the ability to form coherent words, we remain poised at the top of the hierarchy of day-to-day life. We ride like fucking bosses in that car seat, nose to the sky, deciding the fate of lunch with a metaphorical thumbs up or down in every scream of, "NO! Burger King is gross, and you know I don't like anything at Zaxby's!" Once again, you win the day with McDonald's for the eighth straight meal. These adults don't seem to mind, though. You are a do-no-wrong prodigy in their eyes in these early moments of life.

Then comes the real test into the murky waters of what will soon be our realities. That first day into school, be it head start, day care, or for the future home-school kids, not until kindergarten. The overconfidence and bloated air of self-importance we have spent the first three to four years of our lives building up, not really based on anything internally but through the actions of everyone around us, making us the centres of all things, comes crashing down in about an hour. The look-at-me cries and tantrums that would be acknowledged almost immediately are now being met with, "You are going to have to calm down," or, "Be nice to the other kids." Okay…What the fuck is happening? Do these people not know who I am? First of all, Tommy has been picking his nose since he got here, so I don't want his funky little hands touching me. Second, I don't drink apple juice. Did my people not properly communicate this? Next, fuck Cailou! The kid's been bald for years, yet I have never seen any chemo treatments, and his whiny little voice gives me diarrhoea. Lastly, I take naps at my leisure. I can't sleep so close to lunch, and both the kids I'm forced to lay between refuse to wear their socks. I don't know where those creepy little toes have been before today. What is this, an internment camp? I know my rights because my parents have told me and taught me; I'm number one.

Now, once your legal guardians pick you up, they make the mistake of asking you how your first day was at this toddler hell. This is when you let them have it. How dare they stick you in such a place, surrounded by incompetents, herded together like sheep? What's tomorrow going to bring? Are they going to shave us for what little prepubescent hair we have to make a quilt or something? Freaking sickos. Now, trying to get the misery of the day across as a toddler is definitely not artful communication. Basically, you just say, "I didn't like it, or I don't want to go back." There, with such creative statements like this, there is no way any Godfearing and compassionate parents of mine will dare send me back to that place. They aren't Nazis, after all. For the rest of the day, you are treated like the king or queen you have been accustomed to the first few years of your life. You go to sleep comfortable and confident that you will not be sent back the next day. Then the next day comes…

I think this, or at least somewhere and sometime like this, is where we realise that we are not the centre of the universe. If your parents, grandparents, or whomever made you feel like you were this unfaltering, unwavering beam of perfection for the first few years of your life, it is not a bad thing. Some people are not fortunate enough to have had that in those early years, so I'm not here to condemn or knock being treated so wonderfully and lavished with praise and love. I hope I have done my daughter justice in just how much I love her and how proud I was and am of everything she did or will ever do in her life. This could be something as simple as maybe having the most massive BM I have ever seen in my life when she was like four; like seriously, it took three flushes and hung around like a beached whale until gravity and water pressure finally prevailed, or using a Starbucks gift card to pay for a girl's drink who had to pull out of the line in front of us because her car started smoking and then handing it to her out the window. These things, especially for the parents out there, give us a sense of pride and love toward our children that, in the grand scheme of life, is unrealistic or, yes, trivial to most anyone else. The thing that is so hard to remember and recapture starting from those times we first encounter some structured pushback from others that we are not perfect and the most important person in the room is how do we get a little bit of that back in our daily routines. From day care or school, to then organised sports, clubs that we join, family events as we get older, work from our first jobs to our careers, and then relationships with our friends and our significant others that importance and joy get sucked out of us little by little until we become somewhat hollow and start to question if we will ever feel like we matter as much as we seemed to as children to ourselves and to the people that enter and exit our lives. But I have news for you. There is beauty and importance in even the simplest things we do in our lives that we should try and take time to appreciate.

Now, trying to make these every day monotonous routines seem to be something more is a difficult thing to do. There is no way I can convey these in a manner that will do justice to another's perspective but my own. A 40-something divorcee, single dad of a preteen who has nothing figured out and with each coming day doubts himself a thousand times over to the point where anxiety can set in so severe that sometimes it's a challenge to leave the house is my perspective. But hopefully, someone can relate to finding some deeper meaning in some of the everyday journeys of work, parenting, self-exploration, relationships, and just daily tasks that we all do. I may just see them as a real; no one cares about how long I will wait in a sit-down restaurant to be seated before I draw a hard line. But even that matters in the interwoven fabric of how each of our lives plays out.

The first topic to tackle is something that I am sure most people just think is an issue that only women run into. It has been fodder for satire and portrayed constantly on TV and movies with extreme versions of the issue, resulting in fights, a series of wardrobe changes, and in some cases, missing dinner reservations, but finding the exact right thing to wear is not just confined to ladies. That's right; even men suffer the same cruel uneasiness of putting on shirt after shirt or trying to squeeze into the pair of jeans we've kept since college because, "I am definitely going to get back to playing weight one day." I mean, yeah, I'm 40 now, and my metabolism toys with me as if I am Joey trying to decide between Dawson and Pacey. Pacey, really, what the hell? It's called *Dawson's Creek*, for fuck's sake, and she ends up with the emotionally unavailable one. He's the Beeker—a freaking legend. John Moxon, anyone? But no, let her end up with the shitty werewolf from *Cursed*. But I digress. Getting dressed? Surely, I am not the only guy who goes through this daily challenge. I am truly envious of the men that honestly don't care how they look, what they wear, how they smell, or what the world around them thinks of their choices. That is a really free way to live your life, and I don't think I will ever get to that level of contentment, but my god, it would be amazing!

But, unfortunately for myself and for way more men than are probably willing to admit it, trying to get ready to venture out is a struggle. Whether it be for work, going on a date, heading to the gym, or, in my case, just going to the store to grab three or four things can be way more difficult than it needs to be. First, let's start at the bottom. Socks, who cares, right? Wrong! If you have a job where you have to dress business casual or a little more then the right sock is key. Black is a safe and solid choice with most outfits, but browns and blues? Hold the phone! How dark is the pant you are wearing, and the shirt? Are you wanting it to contrast completely if you are a bold guy, or blend in more with the outfit? But make sure it isn't too matchy-matchy. If you even think about white, then you aren't even trying.

Now for the pants, colour being excluded, are they the right length? There are few wardrobe problems more frustrating than when you are definitely an odd length, say a 31 and trying to find a fucking 34 x 31 pant. For a while, I did not think they even existed. A 32, fine, I will just walk on the back of these pants all day until they eventually bore a hole in the leg. And if it's raining, HA! Every time I walk around a corner, I will just do a Van Damme split if I take it too fast. If I go with a 30, that's cool too. I will just be asked if I am a trendsetter for wearing capri pants to a business meeting, and that's before I even sit down. Once seated, you guessed it, now I am wearing shorts to a meeting. Speaking of shorts, just when I got used to them being so long and that being the acceptable trend, now suddenly, any dress shorts I buy hugs my ass cheeks like I should be leaving it $40 in the drawer after I take them off.

Let's move on to the shirt selection. I have a longer torso and a shorter upper body, so after adding some weight for years, I learned that horizontal stripes were not kind to me. It wasn't until recently that I have started back down that path a little. Necklines are a challenge too. I tend to stay on the hairy side, so a V-neck can make it look like I'm trying to smuggle a chihuahua into a building. A thinner shirt with this same hair issue can make it look like I am actively getting acupuncture. Then, the major issue with shirts for most men is whether to tuck or not to tuck. That is the question. This is such a little-explored stress in men's fashion. It is only recently that there have been sites dedicated to tuck-less shirts with sophisticated designs. In most jobs, a tucked-in shirt is expected, so that takes care of our dilemma right there in a way. It is required for 40–60 hours of my life; what a relief! No thinking needed. If you are super skinny or a little on the obtuse side, you can take a look at yourself, and even if you are not super happy with the look, it's part of the job. But for all other activities, it becomes a problem. The gym is an issue. I always remember thinking to myself at what age did my dad start tucking in t-shirts. The answer? The age I'm at now. I wear a lot of tanks to the gym, and it seriously takes me 15 minutes to tuck them into the shorts. Then I think this is stupid—a tank into shorts? So then I untuck it, look at myself and see how my little pear-shaped stomach at the bottom makes my love handles look like the ears on an elephant, so I tuck it back in. Then I go through each of the exercise movements I'm going to do to see at the end of each one how it looks. Did the shirt come out too much? When I start to sweat, will it cling to my stomach too much where people see my chunkiness? So, I untuck again and say to myself, "God, you are stupid!" I then make my way to the car and out the door before stopping by the mirror at the door to look one last time, and then, yeah, that's right, tucked back in. Polo shirts are the worst. When you are in between sizes and carry most of your weight on the very bottom part of your stomach, a polo shirt can be the most frustrating thing in a man's wardrobe. Again, there is the decision of tucking or untucking. If you carry the weight in the front and leave it untucked, you run the risk of being asked, "How far along are you?" and, "You already have a girl; fingers crossed for a boy, right?" First of all, Barry, you are three times bigger than me, so the choice to wear the same black t-shirt to the cookout is so brave. Secondly, yes…I do hope it's a boy. If you carry the weight on the sides, like me, leaving it untucked can make it protrude out like you have natural gun holsters. Tucking them runs the risk of looking too business casual just to go out and also shifts the look to your chest, so, 'hello, man boobs'. But, if you decide against the 15 polo shirts you have in your closet because at some point you were like, "Yeah, it's the fourth blue one, but my eyes are blue, and I'm wearing this next weekend for sure," and decide on an old trusty button-up, then you are rolling up sleeves and wearing them constantly even in summertime weather. That fourth blue shirt still has the tags on it, by the way, from three years ago. But then, with button-ups trying to be casual, you must think whether it's too casual at dinner to leave untucked or too stuffy to tuck in. Especially on a date of some kind. You have to really evaluate if your date is an untucked or tucked person. Also, if you go from one size to another, like lose weight from an XL to an L, a button-up can be a problem. The XLs are way too baggy and long now, so you start buying L sizes, but hold up; it's tight in that bottom part again, so you tuck and then do the 360-degree spin in the mirror to try to look at all angles. You also do an air sit, trying to figure out if once seated at dinner, your pudge doesn't stick out from the side too much. This is all pretty exhausting.

Another issue that I have run into as I have gotten older and my body chemistry is apparently changing is that I stay so hot and sweat like crazy. This can be incredibly frustrating and embarrassing when you are trying to find clothes to wear out in the world. I unfortunately have gotten to a point where I can only wear darker colours or tanks all the time for fear of sweating right through the fabric within minutes. People tend to think the tank part is just something I choose to do out of some misguided vanity to showcase my arms or shoulders. But this could not be further from the truth. If I tried wearing a short-sleeve shirt of any kind to the gym now, I would look like I just got out of the pool after about 30 minutes of working out. It is something that the self-conscious metre is off the charts on. I have tried eight different kinds of clinical-strength deodorants and seen a dermatologist about the issue, but nothing has helped. It is like since hitting 40, my body just had excess fluids, which I built up all my life apparently, and just started dumping them out over the last few years. Sometimes I have changed shirts three times because in the course of getting ready to leave the house, I have sweated through that many. Obviously having to deal with something like these clothing options has grown more frustrating. I would love to wear a bright neon green shirt to go do something in, but it would be stained within minutes.

Hats? Am I right, guys? Unfortunately, the number of crowns I have in my head causes my hairlines to diverge into paths that lead them to completely different ends. It's like doing one of those games on the Cracker-Barrel old-school kids' menu, but all the paths lead to a fucking wall. So, with that, just fixing my hair is a process. I have to wet it, then dry it with a dryer, and then wet it in places again to get some of it not to stick up, and then mousse or hairspray because my hair if the air hits it at all, it goes in 10 different directions. So instead of all that, I will throw a hat on. Hats are great problem-solvers for guys. Hair's a mess, put a hat on. You are starting to lose your hair, it's hat time. Sun's out today, it's hat weather. Heading to a body of water all day, no way you are letting that hair get messed up, so once again, a hat is the answer. It's like the male version of a ponytail holder. Still, as great as they are, you don't always want to wear one to a nice dinner or on every weekend because that's just too much. Then, you must pick the right one. Lately, the only ones I think look right on me are the trucker-style hats. So, my mother brought me this amazing one back from her vacation two years ago. Fast forward to five different ones I have ordered or bought on my own, and I finally found a replacement for it. Some guys are even more particular about hats than that. It can't make your head look too big; it can't squeeze it too tight, can't be too loose. The bill must bend just right. Can I wear it backward too? And does it make my ears look huge? For the most part, if a hat looks really good, we really don't care what it says. I wore a Trojans one for a while, and someone said, "Are you a big USC fan?" Hell no, but the hat looks fantastic.

Now, it is a possibility that I am just high maintenance for a guy. Maybe my own anxiety and weird hang-ups make something as basic as wearing clothes in everyday life a painstaking process. Certainly, as I have been told in some therapy conversations, I may make life a little more complicated than it needs to be. I have gotten to a point, on some bad days, to change shirts, shorts, or pants several different times to eventually not even leaving my house to go to Target to get a couple of things. But I truly think more men suffer from these types of clothing dilemmas that can make you feel so badly about yourself that it can affect your lives at home or at work. As men, we are taught to shake it off, man up, or rub some dirt on it when we get injured. Life just throws you curveballs. Surely, something as trivial as what we wear falls into that category. It may seem like a laughable subject to let outfits dictate how we feel about ourselves or the way society may view us on a given day. The point is that sometimes they do, and we shouldn't feel ashamed or less manly for letting clothes frustrate us so much. Hopefully, it helps to know someone else is going through it too. My side belly is hanging just enough over these jeans in solidarity with you, brother.

Another small thing, or so it would seem, that can be as complicated as anything you might take on is something I mentioned before, and that is just finding food when there are kids involved. Now once upon a time, I was a married man, so throwing a third person into the decision mix can be a problem. Especially when they are just as picky as a child. But as it stands now, being a single father of an 11-year-old girl whose appetite is both as basic as when she could only count to 10 and also as complex as if she were designing a fusion bomb can make me veer off the road into a ditch before food is even obtained. I could just cop out and do McDonald's for every meal every day I have her, and I would gain 100 pounds in three months, my tastebuds would deteriorate, and I would never know what pure joy would taste like. So, I got to a point around when she was six that I couldn't take that anymore. When I prepare to ask her what she wants for dinner, I have choices for her now. I use the term prepare because I can ask her starting at 5.30 pm if she is hungry, and that same question can be asked until midnight if I don't finally give her a time ultimatum. There have been way too many instances where she will come downstairs and say, "Dad, are we not eating tonight?" Then I will gladly remind her that I asked if she was hungry four times, and the response was always a no. But not a regular no. The no she gives is a very Napoleon Dynamite…NO! Gaaawwwdd! By at least 8 pm, now I will lock her down to getting some food. Since the blanket 'What do you want to eat?' always ends in a frustrated 'I don't know', as if I have just asked the most difficult question ever imposed or the golden arches again, I now give her three options. On a side note, giving people options in threes for any question asked is a good strategy. It works for anything, really. Instead of the question 'Tell me something about yourself?', ask, 'Tell me three things about yourself?'. When you lock people into a finite number instead of a broader question, it really makes people concentrate to give you a good answer. It also works for people who will ramble for 10 minutes about a simple question. Asking someone to describe themselves in threes causes the modest to expand and the boastful to retract. When this is applied on something as simple as asking an 11-year-old girl what she wants for dinner, then it lets you give her an option that you know she wants, one that you really want, and the compromise restaurant. She now has gotten to the point that when we do eat dinner, she says automatically, "What are my three options?" When I give these, I am prepared that if I throw the one with the McNuggets in, there is a distinct possibility that will be the choice. So, I have gotten to a point where I let her know that if you choose that, then we will go to another place that I like, so her food will get cold. Sometimes she doesn't mind, but most times, we go to the compromising choice. A lot of work for some fast food.

We do fast food Fridays now since that is the one day I will allow myself to eat poorly each week, but we also do several daddy/daughter dates on Saturdays. This is usually a movie and dinner. But on these nights, she knows we have to go to a sit-down restaurant. This poses a different issue. The first of which is just the overall motivation it takes for her to get dressed, in something that cannot be mistaken for pyjamas, and then drag herself to a shower to get ready to go out. Again, doing this is tremendously chaotic because now that she is a preteen, if I let her, she would stay in the house all weekend. She would never eat a thing unless it's junk food. She would also just stay on her phone, looking at TikToks or YouTube, until she got tired and fell asleep, phone still in hand. If I were a smarter man, I would invent a device that eased the arm tension as a teenager held a phone and charged it simultaneously. Apparently, the anti-shower campaign is the same for girls as it is for boys. I take two showers a day, no matter what, but I do remember the battles I would wage against my parents to escape taking a shower. My daughter is exactly the same way. I almost have to shame her by saying, "You know I can smell you, Olivia, and that is not a good thing." Or I wear a mask and gloves as I enter her room to get dishes or clothes. She usually gets the hint and will finally take one. Once the prep work for going to an actual sit-down dinner is done, then the choosing a location comes into play. The pickiness that my daughter exhibits is only matched by my own, so trying to find something we both agree on is an ordeal. She claims to be vegan now but a vegan that eats chicken, lobster, and beef jerky, so figure that one out. We used to go to Texas Roadhouse consistently, and now it seems to be Cheddars. After a few months of going out to what I like to call 'real dinners' and every time I ask for her selection the answer coming back Cheddars, I implemented the three-place choice again. Occasionally, I get lucky and get a place I like, but honestly, the fact that she still thinks I am cool enough to go out to eat with and then to a movie is more than I can ask from a preteen girl. There will be a time in the not-so-distant future when she will be embarrassed by me, and it will be all about her friends. I soak up my one-on-one time with my not-so-little girl more than she realises.

Something else that is a complete headache, but not a terrible one, is when it comes to being a single girl dad is the friend sleepover. Right after a divorce and you establish what most custody dictates is the every other weekend visitation; it is wonderful. It is just you and her, and for about 10 years, that is all a daughter needs. Just Daddy and Daughter time. This is when you can spoil her to no end, get into the competitive gift-giving with the ex-spouse, and let her stay up as late as she wants. "Mom makes me go to bed at 9 pm even on weekends." Yeah, we don't do that shit, not at Dad's house. Dad is just the best, and we go and do all kinds of things, and I always look forward and count down the days until he gets me. This feeling really does make us feel like an actual no BS #1 Dad, just like the shirt says. Then the preteen kicks in, and it's a totally different vibe. All at once, just being dad is not enough, so the requests for sleepovers start. Now, with mine, it started about 10 years old. As a single dad of a daughter, this is a tricky situation. Look, I know that I am an upstanding citizen who has never committed a crime, and someone else putting their trust in me to watch after their daughter is something I take seriously. That being said, the first time she asked for someone to sleep over, my immediate answer was, "Sure, of course." Then I thought about it a little more. I tend to put myself in other people's shoes all the time, and if my daughter asked me at the age of 10, or any age for that matter, to stay the night somewhere where it was just a single dad, I would, by God, have a big issue with it initially. My thoughts initially go to the worst places when it comes to letting my daughter stay at a single dad's house. We have all been conditioned to the images of murders and paedophiles in the news, movies, and on TV that almost everyone must be capable of that type of act. I know I am not though, so giving the benefit of the doubt to others should be where my head is at really. But this is my little girl, the most important thing that is or ever will be in my life, and I can't put her at risk by staying somewhere like that, right? This is how I think other parents must think as well, so from the first time my daughter asked me for a friend to sleep over, it was uncomfortable to say, "I don't think it's a good idea." After that, the why nots and how comes started. Now, it is a truly difficult conversation to have with a young daughter as to why her friends can't stay the night. I try to explain that it is weird for parents to allow their daughter to stay at a single dad's house and that they really need to meet me and come to my house first before I give the okay. Once she finally stopped questioning it, then it has been okay. We have had several sleepovers with several of her friends and all, but one met me and made sure I wasn't some weirdo. That one was odd in general. Her dad drops her off outside and doesn't even stick around to meet me, and when he comes to get her or I drop her off, she always meets him outside. Months and several stays later, I still have not met him. That would never happen with my daughter, and luckily, she has not stayed with any of her friends who have a single father yet. Once you become the parent of preference for sleepovers, as I have become over her mother, then chaos ensues. The sheer amount of destruction and food consumed by preteen girls could rival even what my friends and I did as teenagers back in the day. I have gone to the cabinet for chips that don't exist anymore, and by not existing, I mean I never see them again until I go into her room a few days later to get laundry and find them hidden under her pillow as if the tooth fairy moonlights as some Frito-Lay-induced entity that will maybe refill the empty bag. This is the same for cold stuff too. I have had to throw away several cube cheese packages and Klondike bar wrappers. The food I can deal with, but what is more complicated is when I have to remind a young girl that is not mine that they stink and need to take a shower. Once they decide to take a shower, I stay downstairs and completely out of the way so there is no perceived creepiness. I will even yell upstairs to make sure they are out and dressed and in her room. An unexpected shitshow that comes with being a girl dad and having her friends over are the fallouts that girls have, especially in a Facebook, TikTok era. When we take trips up to my family's cabins, then it is a real treat because all of the kids, except three of them, are all girls. The gossip train is in full steam ahead mode once they all get together. I usually am the one that gets to deal with them since it seems I can neutralise the petty parade before it hits Bourbon Street. I usually have to put each of them in four corners away from each other to get a rational story before rendering any discipline. However, if I have been drinking a bit sitting down at the river, my verdicts can be wildly entertaining. "She said I am too big to fit on the tube with her!"

My response, "I will be up early to run; I suggest you join me." Problem solved once again.

One of the biggest yet seemingly basic things that most people take for granted is dating. It sounds so easy, but for a single dad of a girl, it has several complications. The first of which is trying to find someone who understands that my time is limited. I get to meet my daughter every other weekend, and that time is absolutely sacred. I have gone on exactly one date in five years, and that was on one of the days I had my daughter, and leaving her with my mom while I went out with someone almost made me feel selfish, as if I was sacrificing time with the person that meant the most to me for someone that I will never see again. To make the matter worse, I had a job for almost six years that required me to travel 250 days of the year, so that left me 90 days that I got to have with my daughter, so (do the math) that left about 24 days to spend trying to date, get to know, and decide whether or not to keep dating someone. That is kinda a tall task. The younger version of me would be content with a very casual fling in those days or be fine with hooking up with a different woman in every state that I travelled. But the older I got, the more I wanted, and still want, something tangible and real. Don't get me wrong; I did go out on a few occasions with someone I would meet in the cities I travelled, but most of the time, that was with the intention of trying to form some kind of relationship. The first few times, I really thought it could work and gave it a shot, but by the third month of one of us living in Tennessee and the other in New York, Florida, or Ohio, it was clear it couldn't work. Eventually, I would tell anyone who acted interested that there was no point in even making an attempt because it would never work. This is the same thing that I had to do when I was back home and meeting people local who were interested in pursuing something with me. Either way, it wasn't fair to the person I was going to be trying to have a relationship with, which is the right way to go about handling it. I couldn't justify wasting not only my time but another human being's time as well. This was thoughtful of me, I suppose. I told myself that I was doing a noble thing by not wasting a woman's time on me when it could lead nowhere. Noble and also convenient for me in a way because it meant I could never let someone in close enough to really get to know me and, in that way, protect myself. So, for six years, I was able to hide behind the thin veil of consideration for others while the entire time never having to worry about rejection. Then I came off the road.

So now that my built-in excuse for not exploring a relationship had been taken off the table, I was forced to face the inevitability of dating again. Date should really be a four-letter word on the same level as fuck or shit. That tended to be the reaction once I started going on a few dates after I stopped travelling as much, so why can't date be used in place of a cuss word? Like if someone cuts you off in traffic, your reaction is, "Oh date! No, they didn't!" Or when someone pushes you in a crowd, you could say, "Hey, date you, buddy!" This might be why my attitude is so dismissive when it comes to dating. Maybe I need to adjust the way I view it in my head. But anyway, dating as a single dad with a career path that now has allowed me to get off the road and form actual human relationships should lead me to finally finding something worth exploring on the female horizon. One would think that; however, that is not the case. Something that I did not even consider when it came to trying to find a woman to date was that I would automatically size them up to see if I would allow them into my daughter's life eventually. Now I am not talking marriage because I am almost certain that I am a one-and-done type of person when it comes to that legally binding, yet supposed to be about love, commitment. I am just thinking about it in the context that I don't necessarily want to be alone the rest of my life, so if I choose someone to have a serious relationship with, then they have to be a good role model to my daughter. I won't even look in a woman's direction if I don't get a good vibe from her. It doesn't matter what she looks like or how witty she is; nothing overcomes the daughter test. Since my divorce, my daughter has only met three women that I have dated in six years. That is not a great ratio at all. I wish I could just overlook the rational side of me that will not even allow myself to go on a date with a woman that doesn't fit into the good role model category. Why can't I just see one bleach-blonde, low-moral-compass woman? I can't even bring myself to do it. I realise not everything has to be something long-term, but the single dad in me says why do it if it is setting a bad example for my daughter? Plus, once I had a daughter, the way I treated women in general totally changed. I was really not very good to women in my late teens and early 20s. I look back on that time now and am totally disappointed in the man I used to be. This was magnified once my daughter was born. There are so many times that I could just revert back to that person, but I then think of some guy down the line dating my daughter and what I would want him to be like, and it is definitely not who I used to be. But I do have to say that the man I am currently, I would be okay with that type of guy being around my daughter.

It has gotten to the point where my daughter is concerned about the fact that I don't have anyone special in my life. This is an interesting point where your kid sits across from you at lunch and asks, "Now let's talk about getting you a woman." It's even worse when she has a friend stay the night and they both question why your existence is so lonely. 'Do you not like women?' 'Is it because you are so old?' 'What about this waitress?' On and on it goes, with no reprieve. I mean, in a way, it is kind of cute the way she is so concerned with my dating life. I think a lot of parents would find it endearing to have their child so involved in their social life. She is sincere, but she also has a lot of Dad's razor-like sarcasm, so it's like a sweet comment followed by a jab. She is a true sour patch kid. But at the same time, her mom will ask me questions about my dating life too and then let me know how much my daughter worries about me ending up alone. Obviously, this bothers me. I don't want my child to have to worry about my social and dating life to the point that it really gets to her. Knowing that it does affect her like that puts some added pressure on me to find someone. It is getting to that time where I will not be that interesting anymore, if I ever was to begin with, really. I am just past middle aged, so the look's part that is pretty important will start to fade. I just switched career paths, so that is probably not as impressive anymore, and I can't dedicate myself completely to another person still because my daughter is at the full school involvement age, and I need to be there for all of her events. I know I sound like a real catch, right? When I start being introspective about all this, I start talking myself out of the dating scene. What woman in her right mind would take me on? I know my mentality toward myself is part of the problem. I have struggled with depression and self-appreciation all my life. Even in my prime, I was so incredibly hard on myself that it made it hard to have a healthy relationship. No woman or man wants to be with someone who constantly needs encouragement. It's not the kind of encouragement that requires constant praise but rather the kind that gets me through my day without calling myself an idiot or just being self-critical for any reason. I am exhausting to be in a relationship with, honestly. Take all that emotional toll I put on someone and then add the fact that I am a single parent who has high standards for the woman that will be around my daughter and that is a lethal combination. But lately, I've realised that I do owe it to my family and to myself to at least step up to the plate. I tend to think of things on a grand scale instead of just simple acts. So, for me, dating is the equivalent of like, well, not a war but like a small skirmish. Something that doesn't wipe out your platoon but does kill your best friend in a firefight. Then you have to make a vow to him as he takes his last breath that you will get the last letter he wrote back to his wife, and you will not let his kids grow up without knowing the sacrifice their father made, so you get them that letter and let his wife know that the gentle caress and warm touch of her worn yet feminine hands is both humbling and tempting, but you cannot betray your dead buddy's memory, and you kindly depart their home and make your way back into the black cold night, knowing that just for a brief flickering second you knew what true love felt like…and you said no. That, dating is just like that.

The philosophy of dating for me is tough enough. As you can see, I am constantly thinking in my head about the extended standards of what dating life entails. The grand scheme of practical dating for a single dad with a daughter is just hard to navigate. It helps to look at it this way for me because large-scale morals tend to take half of the dating pool away. I justify this as some really good guy standard on my part for not even pursuing dating, for it's a more shallow short-term result, which I am. However, it is also my crutch I use to not have to really get close enough to anyone to be disappointed. Once I get past this speed bump that is my mentality down to the general specifics of what a prospective date might possess as far as both outwardly and inwardly, it gets easier, right? Wrong! This is where the list just gets going. Now trust me, I know that I am not going to win any prizes for being the best date. In fact, part of my problem is thinking that I am not good enough and have nothing to offer to anyone. But even the most self-critical person has things they look for that attract them to another. I am no different. There are a handful of preferences, and believe it or not, some of them are non-negotiables.

First, let's start with personality and intellect. Now for myself, these two things are more important than the physical stuff, so that's why I wanted to start with them. The first thing I look at with intelligence is wit. I am almost witty to a fault. My sarcasm and snarky remarks come out with ease if I am not careful of what I say. I try to keep them civil, but even my mother has told me that my words cut like a knife sometimes. Obviously, I need someone who can keep up word jab for word jab with me. If I get on a roll with the pop culture references and callbacks to something my mate did months before the last thing, all I need is a lady who can't come back at me with shots of her own. I think witty banter is an underrated and underappreciated part of any healthy relationship. Therefore, I need it in mine. The next thing I need as far as an intellect is the ability to put themselves in someone else's shoes when debating or interacting with a group of people or with me one-on-one. I love other people's perspectives, and I think embracing differences and trying to understand one another is a crucial part of the human element. So, if I am a Democrat and my partner is a Republican, I am fine with that part. What I am not fine with is my partner diminishing every political opinion I have because of what I believe in. I may not see eye to eye with someone else on a stance, but what I try my damnest to do is at least appreciate their viewpoint. This country is a melting pot full of other cultures, religions, and beliefs, and that is part of what makes it so great. So why would I, as a multi-cultured, rational American, want to be with someone who, if in the middle of a debate, says something along the lines of, "Well, I don't believe in what they say because they are pro-abortion!" First of all, no one is pro-abortion. I hate hearing that from someone. It is truly pro-choice. I am not a woman, and I have zero right to apply something to them that I will never have to face firsthand. So, if the person I date cannot see it from the perspective of the person having to go through such a hard decision in their life and react to this debate with some kind of empathy, then sorry, I have no room for them in my life. That goes for anything, really. I am needy when it comes to sharp conversation, so I need someone who will at least attempt to see my perspective on things. Another trait I look for in a partner is some kind of warmth. Now, I am by no means a huggy, rah-rah cheerleader. I am pretty stoic at times and am not a super big fan of a lot of touching, and definitely not a cuddler. In fact, on a separate note, the word 'cuddle' just creeps me the fuck out. I think it's the two D's together maybe or just hearing the word makes me sweat thinking about having to hold someone so close all the time with all that heat, and then your arm goes to sleep. Honestly, I am amazed and applaud the people who can hold someone all night and get a good night's sleep. Bravo, my friend! But that word being said out loud…chills, literal chills, and not the good kind. So, an overly lovable kind of warmth is not something I need. But I need whoever I am with to recognise that I have had a bad day and provide some kind of comfort. I truly reciprocate this act but have found that less and less women have much warmth anymore. Again, I am not a needer of hugs. I just need you to show that you are human every once in a while. I also need someone who can read the temperature in a room. What I mean is to follow the energy and conversation as they flow in a group or social setting. It is very frustrating to be in a conversation about a gay couple adopting a baby and have your mate blurt out, "Don't you think you are going to confuse the kid?" I know we all have our opinions, but you have to understand the time and place to voice them. I want you to participate, but if you can't offer a respectful, insightful opinion, then just keep your mouth closed. One of my biggest attraction points is sense of humour. I love to laugh and be entertained, so if I have someone who can do that for me, then that is a huge plus. I tend to be the one that is always making others laugh, and you know what they say, the people who are apt at being comedians are the ones that are the most dead inside. If I have an amazing lady who can make me laugh on a bad day, then that is gold for me. I have often overlooked the other features that I might be attracted to for a woman who possesses this trait. One of the last things I look for is just intellect for intellect's sake. I really don't mind what someone's beliefs, religion, race, etc. are at all, but when I can't even form a normal conversation with you on a date, then that is a problem. Now, I am no intellectual giant by any means, but I do love a variety of topics when it comes to a conversation with someone that I am involved with romantically. If I am on a date and the only thing I can manage to talk about with the other person is 'Kitties are good, and my favourite colour is blue', then I'm sorry, we can't ever do this again! There are so many times that I have had to dumb myself down on a date or via text trying to get to know someone just to have a conversation and not sit in silence. It's not like I think I am above having nice, basic talks with someone, but I just cannot build something with someone that can only have surface conversations. The quickest way to get me to check out on you is to send me a text response that says, 'Yeppers', or just 'LOL' with absolutely no follow-up text. I mean, seriously, what am I supposed to do with that kind of message? It's not asking for much in my opinion to have a nice functional intellect. Those are just the highlights of what I need from a partner on the inside.

Now, of course, we have to talk about the outside. I am not naïve enough, nor should any other human be either, to pretend that some kind of physical attraction is not needed in any healthy relationship. I do firmly believe in and put much more weight on the internal things. I have met far too many beautiful women who had the ugliest souls you could find anywhere. If you are ugly on the inside, then that completely clouds your more superficial features for me. I know not every man is wired that way. Some men would date the most vapid, vicious woman they could if she had enormous breasts. Those men have their own issues to deal with because you cannot spit venom in public and then try to swap spit with me in private. The fact is, for better or worse, looks do matter to a degree. What I find beautiful and sexy in a woman's appearance may differ from the next guy, but the point is still valid. All men and women have physical traits they look for in a mate that will absolutely affect the longevity and longing of a relationship. For me, these are pretty specific, and I am not sure whether I have had all of these in one woman before, but if I could find someone with 75% of them, I would be thrilled.

First are the eyes. I guess the old analogy is correct in this case for me. They truly are the windows into the soul. A good set of eyes can make or break a woman. They don't have to be a particular colour, really. I truly like all kinds of eye colours to the point where I can't pick a favourite. However, as far as shape goes, I have always been a fan of big eyes. The large doe-like eyes of Margot Robbie would lure me in and keep me anywhere they directed me to just make her happy. All I have to see is a woman's eyes to know what kind of mood she is in, so they are a must. Hair is also a big factor for me. I love, love, love long hair. No matter how many loves I put in there, it would still not properly convey just how much I prefer long hair on a partner. Perhaps this next story will make me seem a touch shallow, but it will just have to paint me in a bad light. I was dating this one girl when I was like 23, I think. She had this beautiful curly blonde hair. The kind of hair that my hand would get stuck in, and that was just fine with me. At one point, she decided she wanted to do something drastic with it. We had been together for a year, I believe, and I had gotten used to her long yellow locks, so before she went and got them cut, I reminded her just how much I loved her hair. Apparently, my comment did not matter at all in this case. I was working second shift for a retailer at the time, and I still remember the incredible shock of when she rounded the aisle in electronics to see me. She had cut it short. When I say short, I don't mean to her shoulders short. I'm talking June Cleaver short. Not only that, but she had it styled some Flock of Seagulls way. So, it was longer on one side with bangs in her eyes and then shaved on the other side. She hated it so much that she was already in tears as she asked me if I liked it. I think my reaction was, "Well, you don't like it, so I think you know my answer." I know this was not a good look for me, but hey, I was in my 20s and liked what I liked. Despite the girl being blonde in this instance that is also a big 'no go' when it comes to hair. I have dated exactly three blondes in my life, and what those three lessons have taught me is that maybe sometimes gentlemen don't prefer blondes. I have several blonde friends, and they are amazing, but I just can't seem to be attracted to this hair colour anymore. Now to the skin. I like dark skin on women, and I'm severely attracted to different ethnicities. This probably stems from my enjoyment of different viewpoints from people who are nothing like me. I think this bleeds into my romantic interests now as well. I used to do a lot of work in Florida, particularly Miami and Orlando, and the Cuban and Puerto Rican women in those towns used to get me all flushed. Just their beautiful appearance alone would do it, but then you throw in that accent, and I was a goner. I made a lot of female friends in those cities, and for some reason, they all loved me. Now the other end of the spectrum is attractive to me as well, and that would be the incredibly pale red heads of the world. That's right, I love gingers. I said it and owned it. I also am very attracted to ladies that have some meat on their bones. A tiny woman who eats salads, has the metabolism of a marathon runner, and has a twig-like shape is just not what I need. Give me thighs that rub together a bit, an hourglass at the hip, and a chest that may cause some back issues down the line, and that is the figure for me. It's not that I haven't dated smaller women, but when it comes to sustainable physical attraction, I will take big booty Judy over slender Samantha all day, every day, and twice on Sunday. Samantha can't wrestle me to the ground, and that is a problem. The one thing that attracts me the most physically to any woman is very odd and specific. But I think everyone has their pinpointed specific thing that just stands out. Mine is the small of a woman's back. That part right where the back ends and the butt begins is just like the bridges connecting the Burroughs in NYC. It's where the elegant top with all the beauty and charisma starts to give way to the power and determination of a woman. When bikini season comes and every guy is checking out the breasts and the butt, I am like, "Hey man, check out the small of that woman's back." That thing is insane. Of course, this is also the trashy reason that I like tramp stamps so much. So, it has its flaws being attracted to that as well.

Overall, trying to make sense of the most simplistic things is important. The larger-scale ones, like dating, are an obvious big deal, but I think we try to talk ourselves out of the smaller things mattering that much. I think a lot of people are like me and feel slightly insignificant in general, so trying to pick out the right shirt or liking long hair can seem silly and unimportant. However, if we apply significance to these things, then we can allow them to have an important place in our heads. During the mundane activities of life, we can try to get in our own heads about what really matters. If you are surrounded by friends and family all the time, then something like these trivial things are really just white noise to you. For a good number of us who don't have as many social blessings as others, these trivial things can really weigh on us. The stigma attached to voicing a complaint or just having a conversation about simple things can make some of us feel dumb for even bringing them up. We are not alone, though. More people go through these everyday struggles and discussions in their heads than we realise. We are all okay. I hope that more people become comfortable sharing these trivial things out loud.

The more as individuals we think about what really matters to us in a big picture type of mindset, the more we will beat ourselves up over worrying about tiny little details. How can we think about, "Oh no I can't believe I was 10 minutes late to my kid's soccer game." Or, "Once again they forgot to leave tomatoes off my burger!" The fact that we even get worked up over such injustices is comical. I mean there are starving children all over the place, wars break out on a whim, and snow leopards! We have to save the freaking snow leopards! All the chaos and the gall to be worried over a food mistake or running late. How could any rational human in a now so PC society even admit to caring about small things. I am here to ease your mind. Take a breath, pace the floor a time or two, and absolutely have a little freak out about a mild misfortune. If you can put it in the perspective that I just gave you, then you have well deserved that mini childlike melt down. One of the worst things we can do in a functioning society is to hold those displeasures in, especially out of shame. So, let's explore more of those trivial things a little further. Not just the things that irritate us but the things that seem so small but can stress us out the most. Being a 40 something single father to a daughter is the only way I can see the world. I try to be as objective as I can when encountering anything I deem trivial and try to be an empath to how other people may perceive something similar. Hopefully, my perspective can help someone else in dealing with the average trials of life. At the very least, it will assure you that you are not alone in your neuroses.

At whatever point in your life, you determine that you are just too fat and sassy to pretend like it is endearing and realize that it has become a mental and physical problem, I hit that point at around 38 years of age. Now let me preface this commentary with the point that if you are happy and at peace with who you are, then God bless you. The phases in our lives come at different paces and I definitely had a phase where I was way too comfortable with myself and thought that I was fine. I was married, had a really steady job, had a beautiful daughter and a nice home to come home to. For most human beings, that sounds perfect. That is after all what most of the American dream entails. We try early in our lives without really realizing to gain some form of this dream. Most of us if we can hit one of these big life goals, that is amazing. After all, for most men's lives, they should feel lucky to have a woman be with them. We are sloppy, stubborn, boring, complacent, cold, dream killers that really deserve no creature, especially one as magnificent as woman, to accept us and all our soul crushing faults and on top of that, take us as a husband. Take all our deficiencies and then apply that professionally and we are then thankful that any boss or job would want to keep us gainfully employed. If we were honest with ourselves, then we would probably not hire us, much less keep us around for years. We also are blessed when we are given children. These prides and joys are a way to carry on a legacy and a name and instill deep meaning to us as they evolve and grow older. We see ourselves in our children and know that we have created meaning. As for the home, this is something that is somewhat of a status symbol, much like a car, but that provides us comfort and safety. Having a wonderful home is almost what ties everything else together. That doting spouse, precocious child, stable job, and sturdy house are what is supposed to make us feel complete as a man. What happens when that is not the case? For so much to be grateful for and to give glory to whatever God you believe in what happens when chunks of that get taken away, but you have let yourself go to a point that mentally and physically you are no longer the person you remember from years past?

I am not saying that having all the things that are for the most part recognized in societies as the mark and success of a man is a bad thing at all. Seeking and finding those important four pillars is a remarkable feat. Most of us as men and women as well again will never capture all four of these things consistently and hold on to them forever. Life is hard, even on the good days. That means that at some point in a majority of our lives, we are going to fall short of hitting and sustaining these things that we, and to a larger point, society have said we must attain and keep being the true measure of a fulfilled human being. In this large and daunting task to gain moral and societal dominance and 'keep up with the Joneses', we can neglect the most important factor to sustainability, and that is ourselves. The most successful marriages, parents, business-oriented individuals, and homeowners are not the ones that captured all of them at once and then became lazy and lackadaisical. They are the ones that still try to grow as individuals despite having all those things. A marriage can become stale and die when one spouse cannot let the other one evolve as a person and grow into the best version of themselves. The fear is that they might outgrow each other and that may very well be true. But if that is the case, then they were not right for each other and deserve to grow and go their separate ways with no ill will. Two spouses that let the other grow individually can have the most powerful relationship around since they foster one another's growth. A parent that does the same routine with their child that their parents did with them, and their parents did before them with their children will never truly understand their children and then become frustrated and distant when their child doesn't do things they would do. As for a job, one that doesn't challenge you but you stay in for years just because it is steady and convenient is such a detriment to your growth. A boss or manager that does not allow you to seize your potential for wanting to keep you in a position because they just don't want to lose you or worse yet, they don't want you to take their job is doing your evolvement no favors. A home that you just look at as a place to lay your head and has no real value other than what it would be worth on the open market is really of little worth.

I had all these things and for a time I was content. It is crazy not to be because we are taught these are the things that are important to our existence as successful men. But, at fleeting times, I was happy I suppose, and my life was as complete as I thought it was going to get. While I was working so hard to obtain things that I thought would make me a whole individual, I lost track of ME. What I have found as I have grown older and gained some perspective is that you cannot be an individual without a ME. Yes, as trivial as it sounds, I lost the physical part of ME and just gained a lot of weight and became a couch potato and beholden to married life with children and working 60 hours a week. I used that as a crutch to stop taking care of myself as much physically. No time, right? That is everyone's built-in excuse for losing a physical edge. I get it, I really do. For men who are not self-centered and egotistical, putting all of the things such as family and job above their own physical health is noble. They sacrifice and put that time where it should be, correct? Right? Bullshit! If you don't take the time and make the time to take care of yourself physically, then here are some things that will happen. That doting wife will start to notice the extra pounds or just lack of really focusing on appearance and she will find that attention somewhere else. I know this from experience. You will not be able to participate in your child's sports because you are so out of shape that you can't run down a soccer ball without taking a break to eat a box of Slim Jim's afterward. As for your job, when you are physically unable to do simple things, this affects performance in every way, including your job. Even if you have a desk job, which can be a hinderance, lack of having some form physical health can affect your sleep and concentration levels while trying to perform simple job tasks. If you are trying to maintain a well-managed home, especially in the landscaping department…good luck tubby! I remember just trying to use the riding mower when I was like 60lbs overweight, and I thought I was going to have a coronary. Then weed eating! Nope fuck that! I will just spray grass killer around the perimeter. That does the trick. Inside housework can be just as bad. I remember sweating profusely just mopping the kitchen, just like I had been on the stair master for 20 minutes. When most people, including myself, decide to put their physical health in perspective and get it right, it is not for some exterior gain but rather for the functional tasks of our everyday lives. Stop letting people trivialize your health by making you feel guilty for going to the gym so much.

To that point, I really fell out of favor with my health and myself from the age of 26–38. Life happens all the time and that is no excuse for not taking care of yourself. But I understand how difficult it is to once again, as a man, start making sacrifices to better the lives of all of those around you. You do after all have so many people depending on you and really to a degree and as a point of pride, how can you let people down that depend on you? That is an easy one to answer. Once you let yourself down, then the others around you don't really matter. If you put no focus on your evolution as a person, not just mentally and spiritually, but also physically, then you have let the one person down that matters the most in this world. That being you! You cannot expect to be your best for others if you can't be your best for yourself. I am in no way saying that you have to be a cross-fit, body-building, cardio bunny to be the best for yourself physically. But if you were in really good shape and did things extracurricular-wise that helped draw your girlfriend, wife, boyfriend to you in that physical realm of attraction, then you by God better keep true to that as the relationship progresses. Whomever you were as the person that your significant other fell in love with initially should be the person you remain at your core. Of course, we all evolve and change as time goes on and no one is crueler than Father Time in our physical characteristics. Skin sags, belly fat grows, and wrinkles deepen. These are inescapable facts. We cannot outrun time. But we sure as shit should not speed it up! What do I mean by this? If you are going to the buffet twice a week for dinner, you already know the answer! If you play video games for 10 straight hours in the spring when it is sunny and 80 degrees outside, you already know the answer! If your amazing spouse shows up to bed in high wasted shorts and a halter and you tell her, "I only have three episodes of Yellowstone left, move out the way," you already know the answer. The capacity we must be complacent is astounding. Complacency easily transitions to laziness, which then turns into frustration for a couple and then contributes to the relationship ending. Why, as human beings, do we get so comfortable? The word alone lies in the answer. Comfort by itself is considered a good thing. It is in the name of hotel chains, the fit of jeans, and how we describe living in general once we achieve a status where money and time become less and less important. Comfort determines our quality of life to a degree. But I am here to tell you that 'comfort' kills! Especially when it comes to our physical health and appearance. If you ever think you are in a place where you're so comfortable with your spouse that your physical stability and maintenance is of no consequence, then do one of two things. Buy a motor home or some other form of retirement space in Florida and just wait for the sweet embrace of death to come take you together in the comfort of each other. The second option is to RUN! Never accept anyone that accepts you for less than what you were before meeting them or that doesn't want you to grow as a human being, which includes physical fitness. You cannot give up on yourself and let yourself go to the point of gaining excess weight, becoming lethargic, or completely compromising your health and appearance for the sake of finding comfort in a relationship. That is ludicrous, and not, "Move bitch get out the way!" ludicrous. When spouses give leeway to enable this type of behavior, they are not doing their loved ones any favors. You cannot have the mindset that, "I've got them now, so the work is over." That is when you should work harder. For those of you that say, "It is what's on the inside that matters." I get you; I really do. But, with all due respect, you are only half correct. I have not, nor has anyone I have ever known in my life, fallen in love with just the person's insides. The sad truth is that that outward attraction matters just as much. So whatever level you are at when you fall, make sure that is the level you stay at to hold on to them.

We all fall victim to this appearance and exterior desirability complacency. Mine was just as bad and unfortunate as anyone else. When I was in my early twenties, I was so concerned with personal appearance that most of the exercise I did was to that end. I did nothing in a gym or at home to get stronger or feel better. I did it just so I could look better for the opposite sex. This, on the surface, can sound like a very naïve and vain way to go about a workout. If the only goal you have is to attract another human being from your workouts, then you are doing it for the wrong reason. Or are you? It can seem rudimentary and trivial, but to the root of the point, it's kind of true. As much as I love the functionality and good health the gym provides me with when I go on a regular basis, a small part of me does it so I can be more attractive for a mate. If you already have a mate, an underlying factor is always, "Man, I have to do this so she doesn't find someone hotter." Sounds stupid, right? If you are really honest with yourself, then you will see I am right. No human being that has ever gone to the gym or tried to exercise at least once in their lives has done it for purely functional life reasons, or at least until they get much older. In the back of anyone's mind, even the tiniest voice says. "Man, my ass is going to get attention for sure!" Everyone has done this to a degree! If you say you have not, then don't mind me as I stand as far from you as I can in a lightning storm. Own that shit! Be proud that you have wanted to transform yourself physically or maintain what you already have for the attention or approval of a significant other. It is nothing to be ashamed of at all. This doesn't make you shallow or less of a person for catering to even the most primordial animalistic ideals of the world we live in. Honestly, it can be enlightening to realize that, "Yeah, I am a little concerned with how people see me physically." When we take the stigma out of vanity and being conceded and place it more appropriately into proper context, which is embracing a big part of Self Care, then it can be more acceptable for us.

Once I was toward my late 20s and had dated enough to 'think' I knew what I wanted in a potential spouse, the need for the gym life steadily declined. I had met someone wonderful and now they had accepted me for all my flaws and imperfections, so why go to the gym so much? Which, while I am thinking about it, let me give you the reality of the new year, new body resolution that most people adopt every January 2. I say the 2nd because we all know that January 1 is for full recovery of the debauchery we experience on New Year's Eve. I work at a gym as a personal trainer now, and the people that come in for the new year resolution are all pretty much the same. They step on the scale January 2, realize, "Oh shit, spring break is earlier and earlier now so I better hit the gym and get my body right!" Or, "My spouse says I need to lose some weight." Both are very valid and common reasons for starting a gym life. But here is what happens…People come in and ask all the appropriate questions and then a good many of them will dismiss anything I say by stating something like, "Yeah, I have spent a lot of time at the gym before, I think I know my way around. No, thanks, I don't think I need any kind of personal training." Thinking you have all the answers coming to the gym for the first time in 10 years is a joke. I have seen countless big men come in and absolutely kill it on the bench or squat the first week of membership. They do the max weight that they used to do in their 20s and they feel very proud of themselves. But you know who I don't see for the next two weeks because they hurt themselves week 1? That's right, these same arrogant pricks with all the machismo dripping off of them 7 out of 10 times go way too hard, too fast and set themselves back in their training. But back to the resolutory divas. So, from January until February 13, the gyms are packed and those of us that are regulars and have routines, have to sit and wait for machines to not be occupied by the texters, or worse yet the teenagers in their one size too small wife beaters, pajama bottoms, and crocs. The minute you decide crocs are okay to work out in is the minute you lose just a little respect for yourself. Then what happens on February 14? That's right, the shallowest of all holidays. Valentine's Day is the holiday where we tell our significant other, "Hey, I have neglected you and our romantic journey for 364 days, but here are some flowers that will die within a week and I have a gift certificate to Red Lobster that I need to use anyway, soooo I love you! How about another year with this trainwreck?" More times than not when the 14th comes and goes, the gym crowd will decline by half. Their significant other has accepted them for who they are, body and all, so why in the world would we want to make ourselves more physically fit, attractive, and healthier if we already have our mate in our back pocket? That's crazy, right? Wrong tubby! Men and women never stop dating your mate, and never think you can settle for your physical fitness. Always keep being the best version of yourself each day and remember, complacency kills. The ones I love to see come in the gym are the ones that got dumped on Valentine's Day. The freaks come in for that revenge body and work their asses off to get it. High salute and praise for these men and ladies. That is, until they get another boyfriend or girlfriend and forget the gym is part of the reason they are able to find love again.

Your gym life, like mine, should never be compromised. You don't have to go out and join some expensive gym or hire an expensive personal trainer. But do something. Anything else is better than nothing. Well, unless it is like in the movie 'Surviving the Game' or something along those lines. Being physically fit is one thing but hunting down a homeless Ice-T is maybe a touch too far! I wish I had gone to work out more with my dad when I was a teenager. Every Saturday and Sunday, he would ask me to go and even on the days that I went, I would just play racquet ball with the old guys while he did weights. I was doing something, but if I had just done weights early on, then I would be in even better shape than I am now. I did the same thing with tennis. My father would try so hard to get me to focus on tennis because he played in some amateur leagues and could tell just by me starting out that I was a natural at it. I haven't picked up a racket in over five years, but I bet I could be pretty competitive with an above-average player even today. But when you are young, you think you have it all figured out, and that includes your physical health. At around 38, I knew I had to make a change. I was divorced, at a job I hated, and out of shape. So, I switched up my job to where I traveled the country more and because of that, I met some amazing people and got exposed to wonderful cultures that I would have never known about had I stayed stationary in my life. As I branched out professionally, I decided to rededicate my life to my health and fitness. This was very challenging, at 5'8", 240lbs was way too heavy. To make it worse, not a lot of that was muscle tone. I was very strong but not functionally strong. Functional strength is the body's skeletal mass that allows it to do normal, everyday activities like washing a car, mowing a yard, or changing a light bulb. Once I started doing more construction-type work for my job, I realized quickly that I was completely out of shape. Men's pride is a very odd and complicated thing and signing up for a gym membership again as an overweight, divorced shell of himself was harder than I thought it would be. I started off slowly, three times a week when I was in town from my job. I was just like everyone else. I wanted results in a couple of months. Once I realized that there was no way this was humanly possible and I had to trust the process, shout out to Joel Embid, my physicality started to improve. Once I had better mobility at work and was not just dog-ass tired after every 10-hour shift, I noticed my gym routine was getting way better and more consistent. Before long, I was doing weight that even on my best days in my early 20s I could not do. A normal habit takes about 21 days or three weeks. The gym is much more daunting. I tell people for working out to become a habit takes anywhere from three to six months, and that is with consistency. But it became exactly that for me, a habit, only a good one. You know not like smoking, drinking, or shooting heroine into your eyeball and then making turtles fight like cock fighting style. Which takes way longer and the payoff is really not worth it. Habits can be good, and my gym habit has supplanted bad ones like eating too much or just sitting on my ass binging Hulu. Once this becomes a habit, don't let anyone belittle it or make you feel obsessive over it. My daughter will tell me on Sundays when I say, "I am going to the gym." She pauses for a second and says things like, "Let me guess, you had one cupcake yesterday?" Then I respond with an even snarkier, "Exactly!"

One enormous factor that is not discussed near enough in working out is what it does for us mentally. As someone who struggled with weight the majority of my life, I don't think it is any coincidence that I struggled with my mental health as well. For better or worse, people that tend to be overweight or unhealthy develop just as debilitating mental stigma as well. No one really glamorizes the larger people in our society and that is a shame. But that speaks more to what we have learned to accept as just and beautiful in this world more than what should be. I do know that when I was about 40lbs heavier and had an extra love handle, my confidence, esteem, and overall happiness was directly affected by how I saw myself and how I thought others saw me as well. We can be told nonstop that it is on the inside that counts, but when the world around us constantly reminds us that is not 110% the case, then since we cannot turn our fat asses inside out, we beat ourselves up all the time until we finally decide to do something about it. In my case, and what I feel would be most cases, going to the gym helped me. I accepted the fact that society was not going to change just because I was a terrific person and had a great sense of humor and personality. I also knew how out of shape I was at around 38 and that I was not going to be one of those dads that sat on the sidelines of his child's soccer game in oversized sweatshirts and yelled as loud as he could for his child to, "Run and hustle!" So, I did not just have some idealistic version of what society told me it was to be healthy, I had real-life goals in mind too. What I found in the journey of trying to get my body right was that my mind was also following suit. Endorphins are an actual factual thing that are increased with more physical activity. But this was more than that, really. At first, it takes some time to build up an exercise routine and have it trigger motivation. As I built this, I not only saw the way I looked at myself from an exterior change. Loss of weight, not leaving every button-up shirt untucked, losing the double chin, skin getting clearer, you know, things like that were happening.

Something else amazing was happening as well. I was starting to be a better manager at work, was starting to create more through writing and thought than ever before, and the world was not as much of a pit of despair and sorrow as it used to be. I had not changed in any way other than increasing my physical activity. Doing so had made me a better human being all around and I didn't have to do anything other than taking 10–12 hours out of my week to take care of me. That little bit of time had profound ramifications on my life. That is why I implore people now to take some time to walk the dog. Go out and wash your car instead of taking it through the machine. Actually, go in and walk the grocery store for your items instead of curbside pickup. Those little, seemingly simple activities can trigger a need for more and more. Join a gym, but don't do it in January with the resolutioners. Instead, do it when you have made the decision to make your physical life a priority. Hell, go on May 7 at 9 am and sign up. If you go off a peak time, you will hold yourself more accountable and not bale on it like those New Year gym babies. Make a decision and then do it. I owe so much of my new thought process and finally getting back to owning my life to getting healthy physically.

With a change in physicality, something else began to shift. My mental state started to get better. Yes, I know endorphins are a big reason. I understand science. But this was more than just an energy and mood enhancer. My conversations started getting better, I began to think if I was really being fulfilled in my job, I thought about my relationships or lack thereof and how to make them more complete, and I began to write stories and poems. Some of it is just a shift in getting older and changing priorities, but the balance of exercise now cannot be ignored. The confidence alone to just have a normal engaging conversation with a woman was improved. Maybe it does sound a little shallow that a better-looking version of myself can now talk to beautiful women without getting incredibly nervous and coming off nerdy. But I don't care; it was the truth. I cannot recall the many times that I would just be doing something as simple as talking to a female cashier at a grocery store and think to myself, "I wonder if she is looking at my stomach. The bags under my eyes are probably terrible today. Say something witty, you idiot!" Oh, wait, she is handing me my receipt already, "Okay, have a nice day as well." The battle in my head over my appearance and overall physical shape was a constant, even in a basic retail encounter. I am not saying that I was trying to pick up every cashier or attendant that I have ever spoken with through the years. But, as a man, it is so important for us to be confident, charming, and conversational in those types of settings and I had completely lost that over the years of neglecting my physical health and appearance. I am well aware that exterior beauty should have no bearing on internal security, but the inconvenient truth is that it does. Well, at least in this society we live in today. Once I began to feel better about myself on the outside, my conversations at a store went more like this, "My day is terrific, how has yours been?" Insert name of said cashier now. "The weather is pretty crappy, but your nails look amazing. Okay, cool so I will see you every Monday since you just told me your schedule basically." Insert charming laughter now. I am now able to have an engaging conversation with someone just for a regular shopping routine. Now, this does not mean that I am hitting on her, nor am I trying to seduce her, but it makes me feel better about me when I get engaged this way back. Hopefully, the person I am engaging feels good about themselves as well. This is normal human interaction, but it is made so much easier when one feels good about what the other person sees on the outside.

Now I am what you may call a social introvert. I am very standoffish at first, will barely instigate a conversation, and am quite uncomfortable in a crowd. I have been called a snob, awkward, and in worst cases, a douchebag because of this social condition. It is not that I am unfriendly, it is more just a comfort thing, and to a deeper Freudian level, perhaps I have a fear of being rejected, ridiculed, and rebuked. But I am actually quite delightful once you get to know me. It may just take a year to do so. I tell people shortly after I meet them that my first impression is garbage, but my second impression is fucking amazing. When I first entered the gym on a consistent basis, I was no different. Firstly, I was fairly out of shape so my confidence was shot. Second, I had been in and out of gyms a lot of my life and they were not big social scenes. Also, I tend to have the most intense look on my face as I work out so no one wants to bother me. One guy told me, "It's like in that Stallone movie, *Over the Top*, when he turns his hat around backward." In reference to me in life and me working out. So, with all this combined my first year or so back in the gym, I just put my head down and spoke to no one. I viewed it as an extension of a job. I was there on a mission and that was it. As will happen in most cases where you are in the same place, most days at the same times, you begin to recognize certain people. It usually begins with accidental eye contact, then moves to the head nod acknowledgement, and then eventually speaking. Small short conversations at first about weather or kids can then turn into thoughts on movies, sports, or beliefs in some cases. Before you know it, you now have an actual acquaintance, or some would even call a friend at the gym. When this happened to me, I was such a solo guy that it was more of a nuisance at first to have to stop my routine, silence my headphones, and power through a conversation right after I powered through a long set of chest presses. I would low-key roll my eyes when I saw someone coming over to make obvious conversation. Why do they want to disturb me? I still do feel that you come to a gym, not a social club, but now the relationships I have built with people I workout with is a great one! It is the same as meeting people at bars or sporting events that you bond with over time. My gym people make my days better with conversation and create an environment that I feel very comfortable in. Having this unexpected result from going to the gym initially has made me a much more social and confident person engaging in social activities. I have met so many people going through the same things such as divorce, being a single parent, lack of fulfillment at a job, or just trying to figure things out in this life. Most of our conversations are not even about working out anymore. Has it added time to my workout? Well of course. But I account for that in my routines now. The young ones call me 'gym dad'. The ones around my age will complain about the young ones. The older ones will be amazed at the perspective I have in life. Because of my adding the gym to my life, I now am expected to entertain with a joke or to be funny, give relationship advice, or just a hug. Adding physical fitness to my life did as much for me mentally as it ever did physically.

Most people take the arts for granted when it comes to a tangible interest. An unfortunate bi-product of living in the south for the most part is that the arts are even more simplified and ignored than normal. I say arts to include them all such as theatre, painting or sculpting, and music. For the primary focus of my point, we will think about it in terms of the one everyone can relate to on some level and that is music. Music for me is more than just notes, sounds, and words set to harmony to entertain me. When I think about the people I have met, movies or shows that I have watched, or some of the places I have visited most of the time, the thing that triggers me to think back or to remember any of those events is music. Music is quite literally the soundtrack to our lives. It encapsulates the frustration of our morning commute and then triggers a release of emotion with our drive home from the job. It is the rhythm and tempo to how we workout in a gym or do yard work at home. It is the passion and sexuality to how we make love. Music is also the pain and melancholy way we deal with loss, whether it be to a breakup or to, in extreme cases, death. In these cases, music can take us on a path filled with extreme joy and excitability where we sing our anthems of jubilation and victory with our friends, or it can comfort and console us or even break us down further with its haunting melodic tones or well-timed lyrics that cut us to the bone. Music, quite simply, explains it all. Whether it's in a four-minute Kendrick Lamar rap, a ridiculously monotonous upbeat Katy Perry anthem, or a cut your heart out dark as fuck cut from The Cure music helps put to sound what words and sometimes your own thoughts cannot. There has been so many times, especially when it comes to showing someone how I feel about them, that my words just don't cut it. Thank God I have Amos Lee's *Arms of a Woman* to make that happen for me. But so many people do that now. One of the most effective ways to flirt or let someone know that you have interest in them is to send them a romantic song. We have been doing this for decades. Before, it was so easy to just send a song directly from Apple Play; we had disc jockeys on radio stations doing late-night love dedications. Then, even before that, we had poets who constantly wrote and read prose to either relay or capture the affections of another. I can also remember multiple bar trips with friends in my early 20s ending with a terrible rendition of *Margaritaville* being sung from every crevice of the facility. Mike and the Mechanics' *The Living Years* still makes me remember my papaw Ed because it was released right around his death and every time the radio played it my mom would well up with tears. Music tells our story when we cannot form the words.

When people think of music in the South, what do most people think of, honestly? Twangy voices, lots of beer, and broken-down cars or dogs. Banjo's anyone? The music of the southern part of these United States, for better or worse, is most often country music. Now, I am not saying anything is wrong with country music at all. As someone who loves and appreciates music of all kinds, I try not to be overtly negative or critical of any genre. Music is totally subjective, and everyone is entitled to their opinion on what is or is not great music. However...there is no form of music that I have greater disdain for than country. It is hard for me to hold a conversation for a long time with someone that has a thick Southern accent and thinks the South will rise again, much less try to enjoy music that harmonizes these thoughts. It is like a pure nail-on-chalkboard action to me to listen to someone carry on about the same basic tragic premise from one song to the next one, with the only thing changing is which ex-wife or husband did them wrong. That is just for the older country music. That I can stomach a lot easier than this new age nonsense which they try so hard to make more poppy, but somehow comes out sounding worse. And country rap? The absolute worst fusion ever created next to the bomb. What makes my dislike for this type of music so much worse is the proximity to which I live to the country music capital of the world. When Nashville is only 3 hours away from you the sheer amount of country music and country music stations I was subjected to, especially in the '80s, should have been criminal. That is all I heard as a child. I counted one time when I was around 13 of just how many country stations, we had on FM radio. Out of 32 stations, 15 were country music, seven news talk, five pop/soft rock, two classic rock, two hard rock, one R&B, and one Hispanic. I have no clue how one would establish justifying that many country stations in one city, but somehow, they did and we all paid the price. The expectation from anyone who asks me, "What kind of music do you listen to?" with any knowledge that I am from the South is fairly close to 100% country. So, imagine their surprise when I run down what I actually prefer.

I do like to think that I am a man of fairly eccentric and eclectic taste. I like all forms of cinema and theatre. I enjoy literature, especially eighteenth-century British poetry. This is also reflected in my musical tastes. At one work function, as an icebreaker, the person leading the meeting asked, "What is your favorite song?" Now I have multiple lists, with the top five songs of all time filed away in my memory. I am not a fan of basic questions like, "What is your favorite…or what is your least favorite…?" In fact, as a side bar, I cannot stand it when any vague blanket statement for the best or worst of anything is mentioned by someone. For example, if someone says, "This is the best burger I have ever had!" and we are eating at a Wendy's, what the actual fuck? This applies for the worst being said as well. If you tell someone, "They are the worst person they have known!" My immediate response is, do you mean history. Because I think Hitler, Mussolini, and Husein may be able to lay some claim to that title. I call someone out the minute they open up with a statement that begins with 'the best' or 'the worst'. However, for the question posed about my favorite song of all time, I do have one that is on every playlist of mine and I can definitively say is my #1. During this ice breaker, most responses from the predominantly white, southern members of management for this particular company gave the same kind of answers. Garth Brooks, Kenny Chesney, George Jones, Reba Mcentire, and other country giants were of course what most people named off, followed by one of their very predictable song titles. On occasion some rock songs were thrown in. 'Don't Stop Believing', and 'Sweet Child of Mine' were a couple I remember. Then it came to my turn, and I looked down for a second, and then looked up and quietly said, "*In a Sentimental Mood,* by John Coltrane and Duke Ellington."

The collective thought of everyone in the room was probably the same. "What in the hell is that?" and, "Did he just name a jazz song?" were probably on the tip of everyone's tongues. The blank stares and subdued judgements I received just for having a song choice be so out of the box is something that I have grown accustomed to dealing with over the years.

I blame my father really for this musical diversity curse. Every other weekend, I would go to my dad's house as one of those broken home children, which at the time was still a little rare, but in this day and age, it is the norm. I am very fortunate and proud to have two sets of wonderful parents and step-parents. From each one, I feel like I have adapted something unique. My mother instilled in me my gift for gab, and even though I rarely spoke early in life, I have come to embrace my gift for genuinely being concerned, listening to, and then giving advice to anyone I encounter. My stepfather showed me what it was like to be a little bit of an asshole. He was a chief with the fire department, and he was tough. His people would either walk through a wall for him or slam him into one. But either way, I learned that you cannot always be liked and sometimes being a prick is a necessity. My stepmother showed me a person that appreciated and saw the beauty and wonder in everything. She, to this day, still looks at things through the eyes of an unbiased child, which is amazing. She just loves life and the creatures in it. My father gave me my stoic patience, dry sense of humor, and my love of all music.

Every Saturday and Sunday at my father's house, I would awaken to very loud blaring of the assorted LPs he had. Now as a preteen, I was subject to late day sleeping and getting out of bed to Anita Baker on the weekends was not fully appreciated at the time. However, I came to look forward to whatever he had planned next on the playlists of the time. Whether it was Alexander O'Neal, Earth Wind and Fire, or Patti Labelle, my dad had his own musical taste. He did not stay to the norm of what people in the South tended to listen to and he also was open to other forms of music as well. As I got older, he would listen to the cassettes that I would bring with me. That's right, pre-CDs y'all! Any teenager always has some music that the parent just can't tolerate and makes a statement like, "That is just noise." But my father never made any kind of comment about anything myself or my friends brought to listen to as we played 3 on 3 basketball from noon until midnight. We had Guns N Roses, 2Pac, Bell Biv Devoe, and Troop cranked up and he seemed to enjoy our eclectic tastes. He blasted his records the same way in the mornings whether it was just me or all of my friends staying at his house. It was all such good music. All of it was a little different, most of it way older than the music we should have liked for our age, and all of it was terrific. One of my most vivid memories from childhood was just how different and how much my father appreciated so much music, so of course I have taken that with me through my life. Nothing resonates quite like the arts do and music is the form of art that I relate to the most.

Now that my daughter is about to be a 13-year-old wise young lady of the world, you would expect her musical proclivity to be fairly basic. The basic one-note tones of whatever boy band, rapper, or country rock artist should be the only thing she would care to listen to at this moment in her life. While, indeed, some of that is dead-on accurate, for the most part her pallet is fairly diverse. The painful amounts of radio Disney that I had to endure and the baby shark song paid off in the end. It really does swell my heart a little when I am listening to my adult alternative music and she starts singing to Ingrid Michelson, The Lumineers, or Van Morrison. I know it is a small victory, but I like to think that I have molded her into a young girl that appreciates the diversity of music. That has yet to be translated into film, but I will take what I can get.

One other expectation that most people have of you is that you are expected to be an animal lover to the point of it being a requirement. I say that last statement with complete love and affection for nearly all animals that I come across. But, as someone that has owned pets, well dogs and recently a cat, my appreciation for my own autonomy compared to my desire to clean up feces, buy extra food for something that I cannot make love to or take out to dinner, and take an overnight trip without having a sitter or putting people out to come over and feed these needy four-legged creatures, my need to be a productive normal human being has massively outweighed my love for animals. At least owning these creatures. I will still go to the zoo or watch a funny animal video on YouTube, but once I get rid of the ones, I have in my dwelling at the moment that is it for me on pet ownership. Well, not until I am old and lonely and have driven off any woman that has tried to love me, of course. Let me clarify on the cat I have now. This was not a choice on my own, but rather giving in to a woman I was seeing who just had to have a cat. I was never a cat person, and of course, once the relationship was over, she took everything out of the house except the one thing I asked her to take. I did not want to abandon the cat at a shelter and give up on it the way I was given up on, so I bit the bullet and kept the cat. Don't think I did not think about using that bullet to solve the cat problem. But as I said I do love animals and even one I did not want at all, I was not willing to just give up on even though no one would be willing to take the cat from me (I learned quickly that there are either single-family cat households or three or more cat households. Apparently, the world of just having two cats does not exist to cat people). So please don't judge me as a heartless animal hater.

Hear me out though, unless you have kids, love animals unconditionally, or don't want even the most basic control of your life then why have a domestic pet? As where I got a cat because of someone else's kid, I also now have a dog because of my own. My daughter asked me for a solid two years for an animal of some kind. I used to travel 22 days a month for work, so I had a built-in excuse for not being able to have one. Even an eight-year-old can comprehend that a dog will starve for 10 days at a time and that keeping it in a kennel all the time is not very humane. For the cat it was different. They need no humans, honestly, unless it is to feed them, so every three days, my father would go over, put a lot of food down, and give it 10 minutes of attention and leave. If you think a cat needs you, then you are way different kind of delusional. But a dog is so freaking needy and could not survive and have a good life that way. I made my daughter a promise that when I found a job that took me off the road, then I would get her a dog. Since I do anything my daughter asks of me, and I am a man of my word, I obliged that order when I switched careers. There are only so many times you can go to a pound to look and rip your daughter's heart out by not bringing one home before you finally give in. Once we found a suitable puppy that was not $1000 and went and picked it up, she was never so happy. It was truly a beautiful and docile little thing. Hell, I fell in love with it immediately. So, we took it home and she stayed glued to its hip for exactly three days. Then, as children are prone to do, she got bored, it got bigger, and feeding it every day got harder so her interest wavered. I tried over and over to get her to engage more with the dog but as most parents know, that tactic rarely works. It has gotten to the point currently where I asked if we could give the dog away and she replied very quickly, "That is fine." But when it comes to children, any good parent will try at least once to make them happy in the pet realm.

I realized when I finally owned a cat and about two months into having this current dog that my love for pets was truly conditional. I used to think otherwise. I love animals for the most part. I even shed tears way more when a pet bites it in a movie compared to a human being. John Wick, when they killed the dog, I was angered, sad, and confused all at the same time. Yes, they all deserved to die, and I hope they burn in hell. I Am Legend was an absolutely terrible movie, as are most Will Smith vehicles, but when he has to kill the dog, I believed his acting was 110% authentic. More so than his acting like he has a happy marriage. Therefore, pet ownership seemed natural to me. I had a dog before for 10 years and he literally was my best friend. I would have probably saved him from an oncoming car over 85% of the people I knew. So I get it, pet lovers…I am on board with you as long as it is you! I wish I could be like that and just want to have 15 Labradors jumping on me, happy to see me slinging slobber and shit everywhere. For a while, I was that guy, but at some point in my life, that changed so God bless the pet lovers that can do what I cannot anymore. I will admire your unwavering desire to be covered in pet hair and your homes to smell rancid from afar.

I had not had a pet in so long before that cat fiasco that I had forgotten just how much control they had over every inch of your life. The minute you wake up, you have to let the dog outside, feed both animals, and then stay downstairs so the dog does not eat the cat's food, in my case. Then, if you get hung up at work, you constantly worry about what they might be doing to your house or how it is going to smell when you arrive home. To reiterate yet again for any PETA fanatic, I absolutely love animals. I just think I am ill-equipped to handle them anymore. I love them so much that when I get home and let my dog out of the kennel, I feel immediately terrible when I have to turn around in 30 minutes and put him back up so that I can go workout. The poor guy just doesn't deserve to be kept up when I have to leave constantly or have to be put up when my girlfriend comes over because he jumps on her tiny little frame and she complains that he always smells. Well yeah, of course he smells…He is a dog! But that rationale doesn't help and compound it with the fact that the thrill of pet ownership has passed me by and animals are just not my bag anymore. I am very envious of the 9-cat lady or family that has three kids, a dog, a cat, a snake, a bird, and a snow leopard and do not seem to mind all of the upkeep or that no one wants to come to their house because it smells like a circus, or they might get attacked. Those days for me, at least at the present time, I am afraid, are done. But never say never so in the future when I am 90 and senile, I will probably need the companionship of a lap dog. Or, at the very least, a very friendly field mouse.

We all struggle to think that we are relevant or the things we find important really matter in the long run. There are a handful of narcissists that feel just the opposite. That every opinion or thought in their head is the absolute law. For those rare breeds, I am sure these previous thoughts are ones you never think about. If you want the gym and fitness to be paramount, then they are just that, with no exceptions. If you like K-pop and country music, there are no substitutes. If you love dogs and cats, then people that do not care for them are lunatics. You are not the people who I am talking to really. You are so assured of yourselves that why would you vocalize such trivial ideas? What you say goes after all and I am sure you have surrounded yourselves with like-minded individuals or 'yes men'. But for the majority of us self-doubters and reluctant idealists, we probably never voice our thoughts on these little subjects.

Hopefully, this can give you some reference and assurance that why not say things and have a conversation that you don't think matters. If you feel ashamed that you don't head to the gym but don't see why it's so important, let's talk about it because your opinion matters. I love dialogue and being the empath that I am, I will always try to see the other side. But if you are a little too ashamed to bring up the gym because of the perception that it makes you shallow and vain, then cut the shit out of your thinking completely. Tell everyone how working out changes your life. If you live in an area that really only listens to one kind of music but you just detest it, speak up. I mean, do not speak up in a disrespectful way about it. For example, I live in the heart of where country music thrives, only a couple of hours from music city USA. When I speak of my intense dislike for country music, I definitely do it in a respectful tone. I know to respect country music, fried chicken, and Dolly Parton where I live. For the record, I love the other two things I just listed. But if you are African American and live in an area where Hip Hop is the only acceptable music, but you like Bluegrass, then grab a banjo and let it be known. Do not be ashamed to speak up on behalf of and about the arts that you love. Unless, of course, R Kelley is still on your apple music. Then keep that shit to your urine-fanatic self. If you live in a land of all righteous animal owners who look down their noses at you when you say, "Eww, I don't want to own a pet." Who cares? It is our right to not want to have blurry eyes and have our favorite black sweater covered in hair every day of our lives. Bring these things into light for the sake of just getting them out there or for conversation. You may find that you can gain more allies than you thought, and they may even become friends.